DAILY VOCABULARY BOOSTERS

Marcia Miller & Martin Lee

New York • Toronto • London • Auckland • Sydney
Mexico City • New Delhi • Hong Kong • Buenos Aires

Teaching *Resources*

Thanks so much to Jimbo, Eric, and Fred.
You've all been lifesavers.

Edited by Immacula A. Rhodes

Cover design by Brian LaRossa

Interior illustrations by Teresa Anderko

Interior design by Sydney Wright

ISBN: 978-0-439-55435-0

Copyright © 2011 by Marcia Miller and Martin Lee
Published by Scholastic Inc.
All rights reserved.
Printed in the U.S.A.

2 3 4 5 6 7 8 9 10   40   18 17 16 15 14 13 12 11

Contents

About This Book...4

Teacher Tips..5

Daily Activities

Vocabulary Words... 6–95

Daily Vocabulary Boosters Word List 96

About This Book

Educators and scientists agree that repetition helps the brain strengthen learning. It stands to reason, then, that creative and enjoyable repetition can boost vocabulary acquisition. In his book *Teaching With the Brain in Mind* (Association for Supervision & Curriculum Development, 2005), Eric Jensen examines "brain-compatible learning." Regarding vocabulary development, he writes:

> The more vocabulary the child hears from his or her teachers, the greater the lifelong vocabulary. And an easy way to get the larger vocabulary is for teachers to role model it, expect it, and make it part of the learning.

Without doubt, vocabulary development is essential to learning. Fortunately, this amazing process began for your students well before they ever set foot in a classroom. From infancy onward, children readily absorb vocabulary through listening, playing, singing, speaking, and nearly every other interaction they have with their world. Most young learners are uniquely capable of acquiring new words, especially when the words appear in context and are followed up with targeted feedback.

Daily Vocabulary Boosters is designed to help students expand their word knowledge and synthesize new words into their own speaking and writing. This resource presents 180 different words, representing three major parts of speech: nouns, verbs, and adjectives. Each word includes its part of speech, a simple definition, and examples of its use, followed by various ways to practice its use—through listening, speaking, writing, drawing, and doing. By exploring a word through several modalities, children are more likely to incorporate it in their own vocabulary. The more often children use a word, the sooner it will become part of their working vocabulary.

Our goal is to help you maximize learner involvement with words. To accomplish this, we decided to keep things simple. For instance:

* Many words in this book have multiple meanings and uses. Rather than offer an all-encompassing entry for each word, we chose to highlight one common part of speech or usage. A logical extension is to explore with students alternate uses of the target word.

* Words are presented in a repeating pattern of nouns, verbs, and adjectives. The words that appear early in the book are generally easier to read than those that appear later, otherwise, the order of words is relatively random—they are not alphabetized or categorized. To find particular words, you can refer to the last page, which features a comprehensive alphabetical list of all words in this book.

* Half of the words include art as a visual support in helping students better understand the meanings.

* The activities are meaningful and most can be completed in about 10 minutes.

We hope this book supports your efforts to bring words to life in your classroom, and that it will entice students to acquire and embrace vivid vocabulary.

Marcia Miller & Marty Lee

Teacher Tips

Use the words in any way that suits your teaching style, classroom goals, and the skill levels and learning styles of your students. Here are some suggestions:

❋ Preview the words to determine how, when, and in what order to introduce them.

❋ To present a word, photocopy a page, cut it in half, and post the word and its treatment for the whole class to see. You might enlarge the page for easier visibility, copy it onto a transparency to use with an overhead projector, or scan it for use with a white board or as part of a digital presentation.

❋ When introducing a word, invite students to share what they already know about the word and how it is used.

❋ Post words in the same spot each day, perhaps in a colorful frame, or hang them in a special place in the classroom. As you complete each word, store it alphabetically in a notebook or accordion file.

❋ Add words to word walls, class glossaries, or thematic word lists. Or create a display of the words to post in your writing center and encourage students to refer to it when completing writing assignments.

❋ Use the WordWork activities as day-starters, center activities, homework, extra credit, performance assessments, or as a challenge just for fun! Students can complete the activities individually, with partners, in small groups, or as a whole class. Customize the activities as desired to fit the interests and abilities of your students.

❋ Be creative! Come up with ways to incorporate the vocabulary words into spelling, writing, speaking, and movement activities. Use them in simple games, puzzles, and routine activities throughout the day. Link them to all curriculum areas whenever possible.

❋ Encourage students to keep individualized vocabulary journals that they can add to as they read, listen, write, or research. You might have them apply some of the WordWork techniques to internalize their newly acquired words.

❋ Extend students' word knowledge by exploring related forms of a given word. For instance, when you explore the verb *agree*, consider the antonym *disagree*, the noun *agreement*, and the adjective *agreeable*. This approach offers a natural bridge to structural analysis (the study of prefixes, suffixes, word roots, etc.).

❋ Follow the presentation format of the words in this resource to introduce vocabulary words of your own choosing. Vary the WordWork activities to suit your curriculum.

❋ Invite students to share new words they might come across in their reading, from current events, television or conversation, or just browsing through the dictionary. From time to time, encourage students to browse through books just to find interesting new words to share.

tuft (tuhft)

noun

A <u>tuft</u> is a cluster of something—like hair, thread, or grass—that is bunched closely together at the base and loose at the top end.

Our kitten has a thick <u>tuft</u> of fur on top of its head.

WordWork

SAY:	Another word for **tuft** is *clump*.
WRITE:	A goat has a **tuft** of hair on its chin.
DO:	Think of where you might see a **tuft** of something. Draw a picture of it, then write a sentence to describe your drawing.

pause (pawz)

verb

<u>Pause</u> means to stop or rest for a short time.

Each day, I <u>pause</u> at the bridge to watch the fish in the water.

WordWork

SAY:	Another word for **pause** is *wait*.
WRITE:	Let's **pause** for a drink of water.
DO:	People **pause** throughout their day for many reasons. Workers **pause** for lunch. Swimmers **pause** to rest. Name some times you **pause** in the middle of something. Why do you **pause**? Write about one of these times and draw a picture.

ajar (uh-**jahr**)
adjective

Ajar means partly open.

The gate was ajar when the cow escaped through it.

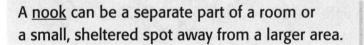

WordWork

SAY: We left the window **ajar** to let in some fresh air.

WRITE: Why is that door **ajar** instead of closed?

DO: List three good reasons for leaving a door **ajar**.
List three problems that might occur if a door is left **ajar**.

---

nook (nook)
noun

A nook can be a separate part of a room or a small, sheltered spot away from a larger area.

Jane sat in a cozy nook of the room to read her book.

WordWork

SAY: We looked for grandma's diary in every **nook** of the attic.

WRITE: They took a rest in a shady **nook** under a tree.

DO: Make a reading **nook** in your classroom. Decorate the **nook** and add things to make it comfortable.

jab (jab)
verb

Jab means to poke quickly with something hard or pointed.

People might jab with their elbows as they push through a crowd.

WordWork

SAY: Did you **jab** your hand with your pencil?

WRITE: **Jab** the potato with a fork to see if it has cooked long enough.

DO: Dance like a silly bird. Flap your elbows like wings. But be careful so you don't **jab** anyone!

dim (dim)
adjective

Dim means not clear or bright, weak. A dim light is hard to see, and a dim sound is hard to hear.

We could hardly read the map in the dim light of our lantern.

WordWork

SAY: Another word for **dim** is *faint*.

WRITE: I saw a **dim** figure in the shadows.

DO: Tell about different ways you can make a light get **dim**. Why or when might you want to do this?

Daily Vocabulary Boosters © 2011 by Marcia Miller & Martin Lee, Scholastic Teaching Resources

VOW (vou)

noun

A <u>vow</u> is a serious promise.

The bride and groom made a <u>vow</u> to always love each other.

WordWork

SAY: A **vow** is a very important pledge.

WRITE: We made a **vow** to be kind to animals.

DO: How is the Pledge of Allegiance a **vow**? What is the promise in its words? Can you think of another kind of pledge or **vow** that a person might make? Write your own **vow** about something that is important to you.

---

shoo (shoo)

verb

<u>Shoo</u> means to make something go away. You might shout and wave your arms to <u>shoo</u> birds away from a garden.

Please <u>shoo</u> the kids out of here so we can set up the surprise party.

WordWork

SAY: I had to **shoo** the dog away from the cat's milk dish.

WRITE: **Shoo** the flies away from our picnic table.

DO: Sing "**Shoo**, Fly, Don't Bother Me" together. Make up hand motions to **shoo** the fly.

vast (vast)

adjective

Vast means very large in size or number.
An ocean is a vast area of water, while a tycoon
has a vast amount of money.

The water in the ocean is too vast to measure.

WordWork

SAY: Other words for **vast** are *huge*
and *enormous*.

WRITE: The library has a **vast** number of books.

DO: What **vast** things can you list? Find pictures
that help show how **vast** these things are.

---

lesson (les-uhn)

noun

A lesson is something to be learned or studied.
Lesson can also mean the period of time used to teach a skill.

The park ranger gave a lesson on how to identify poison ivy.

WordWork

SAY: Today's spelling **lesson** is about words with silent *e*.

WRITE: I take a dance **lesson** every Tuesday after school.

DO: Be a teacher. Teach something you know about.
Which do you prefer: teaching a **lesson** or learning a **lesson**?
Talk about it with a classmate.

Daily Vocabulary Boosters © 2011 by Marcia Miller & Martin Lee, Scholastic Teaching Resources

wade (wād)

verb

Wade means to walk through water or mud.

I wade through water in my rubber boots.

WordWork

SAY: A flamingo can **wade** in the water on its long legs as it looks for food.

WRITE: Let's take off our shoes and **wade** in the creek.

DO: Some birds—like the heron, egret, crane, sandpiper, and stork—hunt for food by walking in shallow water. Find out about birds that **wade**. How are they alike? How are they different?

flat (flat)

adjective

Flat means level, or smooth and even. It can also mean thin, as well as dull.

The baker rolled the ball of cookie dough into a large, flat patty.

WordWork

SAY: Other words for **flat** are *bland*, *stale*, and *lifeless*.

WRITE: Spread the map out **flat** on the table.

DO: An old pillow can be as **flat** as a pancake. **Flat** colors are not shiny. A **flat** soda has lost its bubbly flavor. A song can sound **flat** and boring. Write your own sensory sentences about things that look, feel, taste, or sound **flat**.

limit (lim-it)

noun

Limit means the greatest extent, size, or amount of something, such as a speed limit. It can also mean the border or edge of an area, such as the city limits.

We've reached our spending limit for school supplies.

WordWork

SAY: There is a **limit** to my patience!

WRITE: The raft has a weight **limit** of 300 pounds.

DO: Make signs for a few **limits** you might come across at school. Then display the signs in the appropriate areas. Here are two ideas for **limits**:
- the number of people who can fit in the lunchroom
- the amount of time allowed for using the computer

char (chahr)

verb

Char means to partly burn something until it turns black on the outside. Charcoal starts with the word char.

Dad will char my hot dog on the grill to cook it just the way I like it!

WordWork

SAY: Another word for **char** is *scorch*.

WRITE: I didn't **char** the marshmallows that I roasted over the fire.

DO: When something is **charred**, it is blackened like **charcoal**. Wood can even be burned until it becomes **charcoal**. Name some things that might **char** in a fire. Then use a **charcoal** crayon to draw a few of those things on white paper.

 Daily Vocabulary Boosters © 2011 by Marcia Miller & Martin Lee, Scholastic Teaching Resources

lone (lōn)

adjective

Lone means being alone or apart from others. It also means just one, such as a lone tree.

The lone wolf howled at the moon.

WordWork

SAY: The **Lone** Ranger was the only one of six rangers to survive an ambush by outlaws in the Old West.

WRITE: Other words like **lone** are **lone**ly and **lone**some.

DO: What would it be like to be the **lone** student in a class? Share your thoughts with a small group.

pact (pakt)

noun

A pact is a deal or agreement between two or more people, groups, or countries.

We signed a pact to treat our classmates with respect and fairness at all times.

WordWork

SAY: Other words for **pact** are *treaty* and *vow*.

WRITE: America and Japan signed a peace **pact** after World War II.

DO: Have you ever made a **pact** with someone? Maybe you made a **pact** with your parents about chores. Tell a friend about the **pact** you made.

balk (bawk)

verb

Balk means to stop short or to be unwilling to do something.

My dog will balk when we get to the vet's office.

WordWork

SAY: I may **balk** before I taste a strange new food.

WRITE: My horse will **balk** if she hears a car horn.

DO: How can you show that you **balk**? What do you do?
How do you act? What do you say? Pretend to **balk**.

---

pale (pāl)

adjective

Pale means being light in color or having very little color.
It can also mean having a whitish color, or not being very bright.

My sick brother's face looked pale and tired.

WordWork

SAY: Other words for **pale** are *faint* and *dim*.

WRITE: The stars in the sky look **pale** against the bright moonlight.

DO: Make a poster that compares several **pale** and bright colors.
Which colors are the most popular in your class? Take a vote.
Show the results in a table or graph.

Daily Vocabulary Boosters © 2011 by Marcia Miller & Martin Lee, Scholastic Teaching Resources

ramp (ramp)

noun

A <u>ramp</u> is a slope that connects two levels of a building without using steps. People or things can go up or down a <u>ramp</u>.

Joe uses a <u>ramp</u> to enter the school building.

WordWork

SAY: Most buildings have at least one **ramp** to make it easier for people to enter and exit them.

WRITE: It's fun to skate down a long **ramp**.

DO: Set up a **ramp** in the classroom or outdoors. Roll objects down the **ramp**. How can you adjust the **ramp** to make objects roll farther? Can you control how objects roll on the **ramp**? Try out your ideas!

---

bulge (buhlj)

verb

<u>Bulge</u> means to swell or stick out like a bump. If you overstuff a bag, it will probably <u>bulge</u>.

My pockets <u>bulge</u> with shells and rocks that I pick up at the beach.

WordWork

SAY: The squirrel's cheeks **bulge** with nuts and seeds.

WRITE: Books **bulge** out of the top of my book bag.

DO: Try making these parts of your body **bulge**: a muscle, both eyes, your stomach, your cheeks. Now, stuff a small bag with items from around the room. Can you make it **bulge**? What other things can you make **bulge**?

cross (kraws)

adjective

Cross means angry and annoyed.

Aunt Sally became cross when she saw the mess in her kitchen.

WordWork

SAY: If you are in a bad mood, you may act **cross**.

WRITE: Our grumpy neighbor was more **cross** than usual today.

DO: Write this sentence starter on a sheet of paper: "I feel **cross** when . . ." Then work with a friend or small group to come up with at least five different endings for the sentence.

blaze (blāz)

noun

A blaze is a brightly burning fire. It can also be a bright glow.

The blaze grew brighter and bigger as we added more wood to the bonfire.

WordWork

SAY: The **blaze** started when lightning hit an old tree.

WRITE: The fireworks made a **blaze** of light across the sky.

DO: The **blaze** of a campfire can be enjoyable to watch. But the **blaze** of a burning building can be dangerous and cause great harm. Talk about the dangers of a large **blaze**. Ask someone who knows how to control a **blaze** to share fire safety tips with you.

Daily Vocabulary Boosters © 2011 by Marcia Miller & Martin Lee, Scholastic Teaching Resources

flit (flit)
verb

Flit means to move in a quick, light way.
It can also mean to fly, dart, or dash around.

The bees flit from flower to flower to gather nectar.

WordWork

SAY: **Flit** by, butterfly,
Flutter past me in the sky.

WRITE: The party guests **flit** from table to table to sample the snacks.

DO: Hook your thumbs together, then wiggle your fingers.
It's a butterfly! Make your butterfly **flit** around.

pure (pyoor)
adjective

Pure means not mixed with other things, such as pure gold.
It also means not dirty or polluted, such as pure water.

His green jacket is made of pure wool.

WordWork

SAY: Other words for **pure** are *real* and *genuine*.

WRITE: My favorite scarf is made of **pure** silk.

DO: Many water bottlers advertise using **pure** water in their products.
Talk about why **pure** water is good for you.

dawn (dawn)

noun

Dawn is the time of day when light first appears in the sky.

We like to walk along the beach at dawn to watch the sun rise.

WordWork

SAY: Another word for **dawn** is *sunrise.*

WRITE: The rooster crows at the crack of **dawn.**

DO: Have you ever been awake at **dawn**? What was it like? Draw a picture of an outdoor scene of **dawn**. Or ask someone who is up at **dawn** to describe that time of day.

heed (hēd)

verb

Heed means to pay close attention to or take notice of something.

We heed the traffic rules when we ride our bikes to the park.

WordWork

SAY: Other words for **heed** are *follow* and *obey.*

WRITE: Please **heed** my advice.

DO: Suppose a new student joins your class. What would you tell this person to **heed** in your school? In your community? Talk about it with a small group.

Daily Vocabulary Boosters © 2011 by Marcia Miller & Martin Lee, Scholastic Teaching Resources

sly (slī)
adjective

Sly means being clever at tricking or fooling others. It also means being sneaky.

The sly cat tried to get into the fish tank.

WordWork

SAY: Other words for **sly** are *wily* and *crafty*.

WRITE: The robber was as **sly** as a fox.

DO: Think of a few **sly** animals, such as cats or foxes. In what ways are they **sly**? Describe some **sly** things that they do. Can you act like one of these **sly** animals?

wedge (wej)
noun

A wedge is a piece of wood, metal, or other material that is thick at one end and tapers to a thin edge at the other end. A slice of pie can be a wedge.

All the mice came to nibble on the wedge of cheese.

WordWork

SAY: An axe is a sharp **wedge** used to split wood.

WRITE: A **wedge** looks like a triangle from the side.

DO: A **wedge** can separate things. It can hold things open. Most doorstops are **wedges**. Collect objects or pictures of things that are **wedges**. Compare and contrast them.

thaw (thaw)

verb

Thaw means to melt or warm up enough to get unfrozen.

As the snow thaws, our snowman turns to mush!

WordWork

SAY: Another word for **thaw** is *defrost*.

WRITE: I will **thaw** the meat in the microwave before I cook it.

DO: How long does it take an ice cube to **thaw**? Try it! Put one ice cube on a foam plate. Put another in a cup of cold water. Put a third one on a wet sponge. Do all the ice cubes take the same amount of time to **thaw**? Check to see what happens.

tame (tām)

adjective

Tame means not wild. It can also mean gentle.
Pets are tame animals.

Some tame animals can learn to work for or with people.

WordWork

SAY: A **tame** horse is gentle and easy to control.

WRITE: We rode on a **tame** elephant.

DO: List some jobs that **tame** animals can do. Have you ever met a **tame** animal? Write about a real or imaginary experience you've had with a **tame** animal.

Daily Vocabulary Boosters © 2011 by Marcia Miller & Martin Lee, Scholastic Teaching Resources

skull (skuhl)

noun

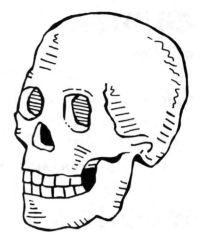

A <u>skull</u> is the hard bony part of a person's or animal's head.

This is how a human <u>skull</u> looks without skin and hair.

WordWork

SAY: Your **skull** covers and protects your brain.

WRITE: Wear a bike helmet to protect your **skull**.

DO: Touch your **skull** all over. Describe how it feels.
Talk about its shape. What openings are in your **skull**?
Gently feel for places where your **skull** ends.

shred (shred)

verb

<u>Shred</u> means to tear or cut into thin strips or small pieces.

Our cat <u>shred</u> the newspaper into tiny bits with her sharp claws.

WordWork

SAY: The strong wind **shred** the banner into rags.

WRITE: Please **shred** the cabbage into small bits for our cole slaw.

DO: You can **shred** carrots for a salad, cloth for a belt, or newspaper
to line a hamster cage. What are some other things you might
shred? Make a list, then talk about why you would **shred** some
of the items on your list.

calm (kahm)

adjective

Calm means still, peaceful, or relaxed.
It also means not excited.

Jon remained calm when his team lost the ball.

WordWork

SAY: It's best to stay **calm** when you're trying to solve a problem.

WRITE: On a **calm** day, the wind is very still and quiet.

DO: What makes you feel **calm**? A special song?
A certain food? A particular place? Doing something
you like to do? Draw a picture of yourself being **calm**.
Show where you are and what you are doing.

dusk (duhsk)

noun

Dusk is the time of day just after the sun sets
and the sky begins to grow dark.

The street lamps in the city come on at dusk.

WordWork

SAY: Other words for **dusk** are *sunset*, *sundown*, and *twilight*.

WRITE: **Dusk** is the opposite of *dawn*.

DO: What usually happens at your house at **dusk**? Who is home?
What changes happen? What do you do then? Is everything the same
every day at **dusk**? Share your experiences with a classmate.

Daily Vocabulary Boosters © 2011 by Marcia Miller & Martin Lee, Scholastic Teaching Resources

crane (krān)
verb

Crane means to stretch your neck to see something. People often crane to see over, around, or under something.

I had to crane to one side to see the bird in the water.

WordWork

SAY: Stand up and **crane** your neck to make yourself look taller.

WRITE: I had to **crane** forward to get a better view of the chalkboard.

DO: The word **crane** comes from the name of a water bird that has a long neck. Have you ever needed to **crane** your neck? Tell about a time when you had to **crane** your neck to see something.

meek (mēk)
adjective

Meek means quiet, gentle, or patient. A meek person isn't loud or pushy and rarely gets angry.

The baby tugged on the meek dog's ears.

WordWork

SAY: The **meek** child sat quietly by himself at lunch.

WRITE: The bear cubs at the zoo are as **meek** as lambs.

DO: When, or in what ways, are you **meek**?
When, or in what ways, are you *not* **meek**?
Write about each situation. Use a different side of a sheet of paper for each one. Draw pictures, too. Share what you wrote with a classmate or small group.

herd (hurd)

noun

A <u>herd</u> is a large group of animals of one kind, such as cows, sheep, or horses. A <u>herd</u> usually lives, travels, and feeds together.

We watched a <u>herd</u> of buffalo grazing in the grassy plains.

WordWork

SAY: The children stomped around like a **herd** of elephants!

WRITE: A **herd** of zebras needs lots of land, water, and food.

DO: Find out how farmers and ranchers care for a large **herd** of cattle. How do they move the **herd** from place to place? How do they feed and water the **herd**? Share what you learn.

remove (ri-**moov**)

verb

<u>Remove</u> means to take something off or take it away to another location.

Some people <u>remove</u> their shoes before entering a house.

WordWork

SAY: Mom will **remove** the crust from our sandwiches.

WRITE: Please **remove** your hat in class.

DO: How do you **remove** paint from a paintbrush? Describe or show what to do. Tell why it is important to **remove** the paint.

Daily Vocabulary Boosters © 2011 by Marcia Miller & Martin Lee, Scholastic Teaching Resources

faint (fānt)
adjective

Faint means weak or unclear. The opposite of faint is strong or sturdy.

I heard a faint knock on the door.

WordWork

SAY: Other words for **faint** are *dim* and *pale*.

WRITE: The flowers gave off a **faint** smell.

DO: Try a few of these things:
Sing a song in a **faint** voice.
Draw a picture that has **faint** colors.
Give **faint** applause.
Make a **faint** tapping sound.

dew (doo)
noun

Dew is drops of water that form on cool, outdoor surfaces overnight. You might see dew on plants, grass, or picnic tables.

The dew on the spider web looked like drops of glitter.

WordWork

SAY: The **dew** on the roses made them glisten in the sunlight.

WRITE: Our shoes got wet from the **dew** on the grass.

DO: How does **dew** form? Work with a partner to find out.
Hint: It has something to do with changing temperature.
Share what you learn with other classmates.

glide (glīd)
verb

Glide means to move along smoothly and evenly.

Swans glide peacefully on the water.

WordWork

SAY: When you **glide**, you *slide* along in a smooth, easy way.

WRITE: The ice skater can **glide** on one foot.

DO: A *glider* is an airplane without an engine. It **glides** along on currents of air. Make a paper airplane. See how far you can make it **glide**.

---

swift (swift)
adjective

Swift means able to move at a very fast speed.

Otters are swift swimmers.

WordWork

SAY: Other words for **swift** are *quick* and *rapid*.

WRITE: The **swift** cheetah can run as fast as a car!

DO: Are you a **swift** counter? Guess how quickly can you count from 1 to 50. Then time yourself with a stopwatch. How long did it take? Compare your time with classmates. Who wins the "**swift** counter" award?

Daily Vocabulary Boosters © 2011 by Marcia Miller & Martin Lee, Scholastic Teaching Resources

arch (ahrch)

noun

An <u>arch</u> is a curved, rainbow-shaped structure that forms an opening, like a doorway or window.

We drove past the Gateway <u>Arch</u> in St. Louis, Missouri.

WordWork

SAY: The bridge support forms an **arch** over the river.

WRITE: A rainbow is a colorful **arch** that can be seen in the sky.

DO: Can you find at least one **arch** around your school or community? Look at doors, windows, and furniture at school. Look at bridges, gateways, and buildings in the community. Take photos or draw your findings. Share your pictures with the class.

whirl (wurl)

verb

<u>Whirl</u> means to spin quickly in a circle, or to turn around and around.

The fall leaves <u>whirl</u> and dance around outside my window.

WordWork

SAY: Another word for **whirl** is *twirl*.

WRITE: If you **whirl** around too much, you may get dizzy.

DO: Put on some music and **whirl** around to the rhythm. How do you feel when you stop? Write about it.

slick (slik)

adjective

Slick means smooth and shiny. Some slick surfaces can be slippery.

Dad just polished the kitchen floor, and it's really slick!

WordWork

SAY: Another word for **slick** is *glossy*.

WRITE: Drive carefully on the **slick** road.

DO: Cooks can make a pan **slick** so food won't stick to it. How do they do this? Ask someone who cooks. Find out ways to make a pan **slick**.

thorn (thawrn)

noun

A thorn is a short, sharp point that grows out of a plant stem. A thorn might also be called a barb.

Roses are well known for their sharp thorns.

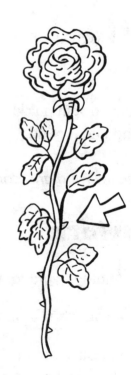

WordWork

SAY: "Every rose has its **thorns**" is an old saying. It means that even pretty things can cause pain.

WRITE: The queen pricked her finger on a **thorn**.

DO: Why do plants have **thorns**? Find out. Share what you learn with the class. Show pictures of plants that have **thorns**.

annoy (uh-**noi**)
verb

Annoy means to bother or make someone angry, or get on their nerves.

I annoy my sister when I sing silly songs.

WordWork

SAY: Too many TV commercials really **annoy** me.

WRITE: Does my music **annoy** you?

DO: Some sounds **annoy** people and make them feel grumpy. Water dripping in a sink might **annoy** some people. What sounds really **annoy** you? Make a list.

gruff (gruhf)
adjective

Gruff means rough or rude. It can also mean grumpy or cross.

The well-dressed man at the counter has very gruff manners.

WordWork

SAY: Put together parts of the way **gr**umpy and **r**o**ugh** sound to help you remember what **gruff** means.

WRITE: The coach called out the plays in a **gruff** voice.

DO: When speaking in a **gruff** voice, the speaker may sound hoarse, like he or she has a sore throat. Read *The Three Billy Goats **Gruff***. Then take the role of one of the goats. Say its speaking parts in a **gruff** voice.

pleasure (plezh-er)

noun

Pleasure means feeling great happiness or enjoyment.

Have you ever received a gift that gave you great pleasure?

WordWork

SAY: Another word for **pleasure** is *delight*.

WRITE: Swimming on a hot, summer day can be a **pleasure**.

DO: Make a collage about things that give you **pleasure**. Cut out pictures of people, places, or things. Glue your pictures to the collage. Also draw colorful designs that add to the **pleasure** expressed in the collage.

---

commence (kuh-mens)

verb

Commence means to begin or start.

Our meeting will commence right after lunch.

WordWork

SAY: To **commence** means to get under way.

WRITE: Now that everyone is here, we can **commence** with the game.

DO: How does your school day **commence**?
How does a kickball game **commence**?
How do you **commence** solving a crossword puzzle?
Share your ideas with a classmate—decide how you will **commence**!

Daily Vocabulary Boosters © 2011 by Marcia Miller & Martin Lee, Scholastic Teaching Resources

moist (moist)

adjective

Moist means just a little wet. Other words used for moist are *damp* and *soggy*.

The dew made the ground soft and moist.

WordWork

SAY: A **moist** cloth on your head can help soothe a fever.

WRITE: Wipe the table with a **moist** sponge.

DO: How is **moist** soil good for plant growth? Explain your answer to a classmate. Talk about ways soil might get **moist**.

spine (spīne)

noun

A spine is a backbone. It is also the back part of a book that's labeled with the title and author's name.

Please put the book on the shelf so that we can read its spine.

WordWork

SAY: Your **spine** is made of the bones that run from your neck down the middle of your back.

WRITE: My **spine** supports my body and helps me sit and stand upright.

DO: Reach behind you and touch your **spine**. Can you feel the small bones that make up your **spine**? How do you think your body would look without a **spine**? Draw a picture to share with others.

burst (burst)

verb

Burst means to suddenly break open or come apart.
Something might burst when pressure builds up inside it.

It's fun to burst water balloons on the sidewalk.

WordWork

SAY: Another word for **burst** is *explode*.

WRITE: When things **burst**, you may hear a loud noise.

DO: Fill a *piñata*—a papier-mâché figure—with treats and toys. Hang it in an open area, then try to **burst** it open. What will you use to hit the piñata? How many swings will it take to **burst** it? Guess and see!

---

vivid (viv-id)

adjective

Vivid means bright in color or light. It can
also mean lively or realistic.

The artist used vivid colors in her work.

WordWork

SAY: Other words for **vivid** are *strong*, *sharp*, and *clear*.

WRITE: The book tells a **vivid** story of jungle life.

DO: Do you have a **vivid** imagination? Use it to tell a **vivid** story or paint a **vivid** picture. Or, make up a **vivid** dance or use a **vivid** voice to sing a spirited song.

swamp (swomp)

noun

A swamp is a place where the ground is wet, soft, and spongy. It is a type of wetland.

We took a boat tour of the swamp.

WordWork

SAY: Okefenokee is the biggest **swamp** in North America. It is located in Georgia.

WRITE: Other words for **swamp** are *bog* and *marsh*.

DO: What kinds of things live in a **swamp**? Do some research to find out. Make a list. Print out or draw pictures of things living in a **swamp** to share with the class.

trudge (truhj)

verb

Trudge means to walk in a slow, tired way.

After playing in the creek, we had to trudge back up the hill to our cabin.

WordWork

SAY: Another word for **trudge** is *plod*.

WRITE: On winter days, we **trudge** through the snow to our bus stop.

DO: When you **trudge**, your feet feel heavy and moving along is tiresome. Pretend to **trudge** through mud, snow, water, or sand. Why is it so hard to **trudge** through these conditions?

tidy (tī-dē)
adjective

Tidy means neat and in order.

My brother's sock drawer is very tidy.

WordWork

SAY: Another word for **tidy** is *orderly*.

WRITE: Dad's office is very clean and **tidy**.

DO: It's easy to find things in a **tidy** desk. Is your desk as **tidy** as it can be? Take time to make it **tidy**.

---

prop (prop)
noun

A prop is any object that an actor carries or uses in a play or movie. Costumes and scenery are not called props.

What prop do you need to play the role of a judge?

WordWork

SAY: **Prop** is short for *property*.

WRITE: We need a wagon as a **prop** for our play.

DO: Set up a simple stage area with only a chair for a **prop**.
Work with a partner or small group to make up a short skit.
Use the chair as a **prop** in your skit. Then perform the skit for others.

Daily Vocabulary Boosters © 2011 by Marcia Miller & Martin Lee, Scholastic Teaching Resources

scowl (skoul)
verb

Scowl means to make a mean or angry face, or to show that you're not pleased about something.

I scowl when we have liver for dinner.

WordWork

SAY: Some people **scowl** when they feel grumpy or annoyed.

WRITE: Dad will **scowl** when he sees the mess I made!

DO: When you **scowl**, you frown and wrinkle your brow. Use a mirror to practice **scowling**. Then have a contest with a friend! Take turns naming things that you usually **scowl** about, then **scowl** to prove it. Keep playing until the first person breaks into laughter instead of **scowling**.

damp (damp)
adjective

Damp means slightly wet or soggy.

The damp cellar has a musty smell.

WordWork

SAY: Another word for **damp** is *moist*.

WRITE: The laundry is too **damp** to fold.

DO: What is **damp** weather like?
How does it feel to wear **damp** clothes?
Talk about how things might get **damp** and how to make them dry.

oath (ōth)

noun

An <u>oath</u> is a very serious promise. Often, an <u>oath</u> is a promise about the way you will act or behave. In court, people take an <u>oath</u> to tell the truth.

The police chief took an <u>oath</u> to protect the people in our town.

WordWork

SAY: Other words for **oath** are *pledge* and *vow*.

WRITE: Doctors take an **oath** to help people.

DO: Use the Internet to find the words to the **oath** of office for a mayor, governor, or another government office-holder. Share the words of the **oath** with a small group. Talk about what the **oath** means.

---

mend (mend)

verb

<u>Mend</u> means to fix something so it works again. <u>Mend</u> also means to get better over time.

My aunt will <u>mend</u> the hole in my favorite jeans.

WordWork

SAY: When will my broken arm finally **mend**?

WRITE: I can **mend** the broken mug with some strong glue.

DO: What kinds of tools are used to **mend** things? Make a list. Did you ever **mend** anything? Tell a classmate about it.

Daily Vocabulary Boosters © 2011 by Marcia Miller & Martin Lee, Scholastic Teaching Resources

oral (awr-uhl)

adjective

Oral means involving the mouth or speech. A person might go to a dentist for an oral check-up, or give an oral report to a large group.

The dentist checked for cavities during my oral exam.

WordWork

SAY: Our dog knows five **oral** commands.

WRITE: A dentist cares for your **oral** health.

DO: Use a recorder to do an **oral** history project on an adult in your family or school. Turn on the recorder and ask the adult to talk about his or her childhood and an important time in his or her life. Give an **oral** report about what you learned.

---

errand (er-uhnd)

noun

An errand is a short, quick trip that is made to drop off or pick up something. A person might run an errand to drop off a message or pick up a package for someone else.

I have one more errand to do before I can go to the park.

WordWork

SAY: Other words for **errand** are *task* and *assignment*.

WRITE: Mr. Jones sent me on an **errand** to the principal's office.

DO: Have you ever run an **errand** for someone? What did you do on the **errand**? What kind of **errand** would you like to do? Use your imagination! Then write about your **errand** and any adventures you had along the way.

drift (drift)

verb

Drift means to move along without direction. Something might drift in the wind or water. People might drift by wandering from one place to another.

Autumn leaves drift in the wind.

WordWork

SAY: Your mind can **drift** when you daydream.

WRITE: Guests **drift** in and out of the room where a party is held.

DO: Build a raft. Use string and toothpicks, straws, twigs, or craft sticks. Then watch it **drift** in a large tub of water or a puddle.

zesty (zest-ē)

adjective

Zesty means full of energy, excitement, or flavor. Zesty people enjoy life.

My zesty grandma was the first one to get in the canoe.

WordWork

SAY: Another word for **zesty** is *spicy*.

WRITE: Hot peppers are too **zesty** for me.

DO: Salsa is a **zesty** food. List some other **zesty** foods. Then take a class vote. How many people like each **zesty** food? Which **zesty** food is the class favorite? Graph the results and talk about them.

Daily Vocabulary Boosters © 2011 by Marcia Miller & Martin Lee, Scholastic Teaching Resources

notch (noch)
noun

A notch is a small V-shaped cut in something. A notch is also one of the holes in a belt where the buckle is fastened.

He needs another notch in his belt to make it fit.

WordWork

SAY: Other words for **notch** are *nick* and *cut*.

WRITE: The handle for my kite string has a **notch** at each end.

DO: "Top-**notch**" is an expression that means the best. People once used sticks for measuring. They made a **notch** in the stick to show how tall something was. Why would being "top-**notch**" be a good thing? Talk about it with classmates.

plead (plēd)
verb

Plead means to ask for something in a very serious way.

I will plead for more time to finish my assignment.

WordWork

SAY: Another word for **plead** is *beg*.

WRITE: Parents **plead** with their kids to be careful when riding their bikes.

DO: In *The Wizard of Oz*, Dorothy had to **plead** with Miss Elvira Gultch. Dorothy was trying to protect Toto. When you **plead**, you argue hard for something you want or need. Think of something you would **plead** for. Act out what you would say or do.

unique (yoo-**nēk**)
adjective

Unique means rare, unusual, or special.
Unique means that there is nothing like it.

The kiwi is a unique bird—it doesn't have wings!

WordWork

SAY: An expression for **unique** is "one of a kind."

WRITE: That singer has a **unique** voice.

DO: Have you played with any **unique** toys?
Have you seen any **unique** animals?
Think of something that is **unique**. Describe it.
Tell why it is one of a kind.

badge (baj)
noun

A badge is a special pin or ribbon you wear to show
that you belong to a group. It can also mean that you
have done something special.

A badge may have a picture, name, or message on it.

WordWork

SAY: Her work **badge** shows her name and photograph.

WRITE: The police officer wears a silver **badge**.

DO: Who wears **badges**? Make a list. Find pictures of a variety of **badges**.
How are the **badges** alike? How are they different?

Daily Vocabulary Boosters © 2011 by Marcia Miller & Martin Lee, Scholastic Teaching Resources

cease (sēs)

verb

Cease means to stop or come to an end.

I wonder when the rain will cease.

WordWork

SAY: Other words for **cease** are *halt* and *end*.

WRITE: Mom asked us to **cease** our argument.

DO: What are some signs or signals that mean to **cease**?
Draw or act out some of them.

---

plump (pluhmp)

adjective

Plump means round and full. Other words
for plump are *chubby*, *fleshy*, and *fat*.

We picked some plump, sweet blueberries to use in our pies.

WordWork

SAY: Uncle Arnold carved the **plump** turkey.

WRITE: The baby has such **plump** cheeks!

DO: Why do you think people like **plump** pillows or cushions?
Share your thoughts with classmates.

youth (yooth)

noun

Youth means being or appearing young. It is also the time of a person's life between childhood and being an adult. A youth is a young person.

As a youth, my dad delivered newspapers in his neighborhood.

WordWork

SAY: The future belongs to the **youth** of today.

WRITE: Gramps still has the energy he had in his **youth**.

DO: Some communities have clubs or centers just for **youth**. What activities might take place there? Make a list.

fling (fling)

verb

Fling means to throw with force, using a quick arm movement. When you fling something, it usually flies through the air.

Let's fling these seeds into the yard for the wild birds.

WordWork

SAY: Two other words for **fling** are *hurl* and *toss*.

WRITE: **Fling** your books onto the sofa, and we'll go get a snack.

DO: Go outside to an open field. **Fling** a ball or a stick as far as you can. What parts of your body do you use?

brief (brēf)

adjective

Brief means lasting only a short time. Brief also means using few words, as in a brief note.

I made a brief stop at the library to pick up a book.

WordWork

SAY: Other words for **brief** are *short* and *quick*.

WRITE: I had a **brief** dizzy spell.

DO: Write a **brief** message to a friend. Prepare a **brief** speech about being fair, then present your speech to a small group. Take a **brief** walk around the room.

purchase (**pur**-chuhs)

noun

A purchase is something that has been bought.

I made a great purchase at the shoe store!

WordWork

SAY: Dad tried on several shirts before he made his **purchase**.

WRITE: I left my **purchase** on the table by the door.

DO: Draw a picture of a **purchase** you've made lately. Write about what you did to make the **purchase**.

fret (fret)

verb

Fret means to worry. When you fret, you may get upset or feel annoyed.

Let's not fret over the dirty dishes in the sink.

WordWork

SAY: Many drivers **fret** when they get stuck in traffic.

WRITE: Don't **fret** if we're not there right on time.

DO: What makes you **fret**? Do you **fret** about school? Do you **fret** about your chores? Draw a picture of how you look when you **fret**.

bulky (buhl-kē)

adjective

Bulky means large or taking up a lot of space. Something that is bulky might have a large, odd shape and be difficult to handle.

The movers tried to fit the bulky chair through the door.

WordWork

SAY: A **bulky** object might also be called *awkward* or *clumsy*.

WRITE: The small gift came in a large **bulky** box.

DO: Fill a large plastic or paper bag with items to make it **bulky**. Is the **bulky** bag heavy? Are all **bulky** packages heavy? Explain.

core (kohr)

noun

Core means the very center of something—like an apple core. It can also mean the central and most important part of something.

The horse eats the whole apple, even the core.

WordWork

SAY: The **core** of a baseball is made of cork or rubber.

WRITE: The **core** of education is reading and math.

DO: "He was rotten through to the **core**." What do you think this saying means? Talk about it with a few classmates.

crush (krush)

verb

Crush means to press or squeeze something so hard that it breaks or changes shape.

We always crush the plastic bottles that we recycle.

WordWork

SAY: Other words for **crush** are *smash* or *squash*.

WRITE: The monkey used a rock to **crush** the nuts.

DO: We **crush** many foods so we can eat them. To make peanut butter, we **crush** peanuts. To make flour, we **crush** wheat. To make cider, we **crush** apples. **Crush** some crackers, cookies, cereal, or other foods, then have a **crush** feast!

basic (bā-sik)

adjective

Basic means something in its simplest form or lowest level. Basic also means at the center, or the most important. A basic goal is to be good to others.

Counting is a basic part of math.

WordWork

SAY: The **basic** rules of checkers are very easy.

WRITE: Tell me the **basic** idea of the story.

DO: In math, the times tables are also called **basic** facts. Practice **basic** facts to help build your speed in multiplication. Then hold a friendly competition to test your knowledge of **basic** multiplication facts.

---

selection (si-**lek**-shuhn)

noun

A selection is a choice, like a selection of a birthday gift. It can also be a group of things from which a choice is made. You might choose from a selection of cereals.

Dad liked my selection of colors for the doghouse.

WordWork

SAY: The menu offers a wide **selection** of desserts.

WRITE: My **selection** is rice pudding.

DO: Practice ordering from a menu. First, look at the **selection** of foods for the starters, main courses, drinks, and desserts. Then make a **selection** from each section. Tell why you made each **selection**.

Daily Vocabulary Boosters © 2011 by Marcia Miller & Martin Lee, Scholastic Teaching Resources

depart (di-parht)
verb

Depart means to go away, usually on a trip.

What time does the bus depart?

WordWork

SAY: Another word for **depart** is *leave*.

WRITE: I hope our plane will **depart** on time.

DO: How can you know when buses, trains, boats, or planes **depart**? You can check a schedule. Look at some schedules. Find different times that a vehicle will **depart** today.

---

jagged (jag-id)
adjective

Jagged means rough or uneven and having points or spikes. Broken glass often has a jagged edge.

The small saw in my tool kit has a sharp, jagged edge.

WordWork

SAY: Another word for **jagged** is spiky.

WRITE: The bread knife has a **jagged** blade.

DO: **Jagged** edges are often made of many notches. They may have a zigzag look. A pair of pinking shears is a special kind of scissors that are used to cut **jagged** edges. Cut some paper with pinking shears. Make something with the **jagged** pieces.

fang (fang)

noun

A <u>fang</u> is a long, sharp, pointed tooth.

The polar bear growled and showed off its <u>fangs</u>.

WordWork

SAY: A wolf uses its **fangs** to bite into and tear its food.

WRITE: Some snakes have poison in their **fangs**.

DO: Collect and display pictures of animals that have **fangs**. Can you point out their **fangs**? How does each kind of animal use its **fangs**?

---

cuddle (kuhd-l)

verb

<u>Cuddle</u> means to hug something close in your arms in a gentle, sweet way. It also means to curl up with someone or something in a close, snug way.

I like to <u>cuddle</u> my kittens as they sleep.

WordWork

SAY: Most babies like it when you **cuddle** them.

WRITE: I watched the puppies **cuddle** together near the fireplace.

DO: Use a stuffed animal to act out how to **cuddle**. When do you like to **cuddle**? Do you **cuddle** with a special toy, blanket, pillow, or pet? Share your experience with others.

hollow (hol-ō)

adjective

Hollow things are empty inside. Hollow things have only air and open space in the middle.

The chipmunk ran into a hollow opening in the tree trunk.

WordWork

SAY: The playground has a **hollow** tube for crawling in.

WRITE: The fox hid in a **hollow** log.

DO: "Freddie eats so much, he must have a **hollow** leg!"
What does this funny saying mean?
Why is a drinking straw **hollow**?
Talk about these questions with a few classmates.

feast (fēst)

noun

A feast is a large meal, usually with many different foods. Sometimes a feast is prepared for a special celebration or holiday.

We enjoyed a huge feast at our family reunion.

WordWork

SAY: Another word for **feast** is *banquet*.

WRITE: Our Thanksgiving dinner was a real **feast**.

DO: What foods would you like to eat at a **feast**?
Work with a small group to make a mural of a **feast**.
Include many kinds of foods. What decorations would you have for a **feast**?

mumble (**mum**-buhl)

verb

Mumble means to speak so quietly that others can hardly hear you. When you mumble, you hardly open your mouth.

I mumble and groan every time dad tells me to clean my room.

WordWork

SAY: Another word for **mumble** is *mutter*.

WRITE: The shy child will only **mumble** in class.

DO: You can **mumble** to say the word *mumble*! Try it! Play a game with a partner. **Mumble** a word. Have your partner guess what you **mumble**. Take turns playing the **mumble** game.

cozy (**cō**-zē)

adjective

Cozy means warm, comfortable, and snug.

I snuggle up with my cozy blanket when I read at night.

WordWork

SAY: The small cabin felt **cozy** and welcoming.

WRITE: My fuzzy pajamas keep me **cozy** in bed.

DO: Do you have a **cozy** spot at home or school that you like to visit? What makes it **cozy** there? Write a poem or story about a **cozy** spot. The **cozy** spot can be real or made-up.

Daily Vocabulary Boosters © 2011 by Marcia Miller & Martin Lee, Scholastic Teaching Resources

habit (hab-it)

noun

A <u>habit</u> is something you do over and over again. When you have a <u>habit</u>, you often do it without even thinking about it.

I have a <u>habit</u> of biting my fingernails.

WordWork

SAY: Other words for **habit** are *routine* and *custom*.

WRITE: A bad **habit** can be hard to break.

DO: Most people have good **habits** and bad **habits**. Make a chart with two columns. List some good **habits** in one column. List some bad **habits** in the other column.

agree (uh-grē)

verb

<u>Agree</u> means to say "yes." You might <u>agree</u> to rake the leaves after school. <u>Agree</u> also means to have the same thoughts, feelings, or opinions.

Let's shake hands and <u>agree</u> to meet each week for lunch.

WordWork

SAY: The saying "to see eye to eye" means to **agree**.

WRITE: I **agree** with you that the movie was sad.

DO: Pick a partner and each of you add 237 + 486. Do your sums **agree**? Do you both **agree** that you have the same favorite movie? Talk about some things that you both **agree** on.

sluggish (**sluhg**-ish)

adjective

Sluggish means slow-moving or not lively.
You may be active one day and sluggish the next.

I feel sluggish today because I went to bed late last night.

WordWork

SAY: The **sluggish** drain is causing water to stand in the sink.

WRITE: When I feel **sluggish**, I just want to lie around all day.

DO: The word **sluggish** gets its meaning from a kind of animal.
The slug is a snail-like animal that does not have a shell.
Slugs move very slowly. Research information about how slugs
move to learn more about what it means to be **sluggish**.

---

zilch (zilch)

noun

Zilch means nothing. Zilch is not a serious word.
It's a fun word.

How much money is in my piggy bank? Zilch!

WordWork

SAY: Another fun word for **zilch** is *zip*.

WRITE: I was hungry, but there was **zilch** to eat.

DO: **Zilch** can also mean zero. Learn to say **zilch** in other
languages. In Spanish, you can say *nada*. In Italian,
you can say *nulla*.

Daily Vocabulary Boosters © 2011 by Marcia Miller & Martin Lee, Scholastic Teaching Resources

reveal (ri-vēl)

verb

Reveal means to bring something into view or cause it to be seen. It also means to make something known, like a secret or other unknown information.

What will the magician reveal when he takes away the scarf?

WordWork

SAY: "Bring to light" means to **reveal** something.

WRITE: Don't **reveal** our secret word!

DO: When you take off a mask, you **reveal** your face. What other ways can you hide who you are until you are ready to **reveal** yourself? Share your ideas with others.

---

eager (ē-ger)

adjective

Eager means wanting or anxious to have or do something very much.

Some students are eager to go to school every day!

WordWork

SAY: Another word for **eager** is *excited*.

WRITE: I am **eager** to make things with clay.

DO: Are you an "**eager** beaver?" **Eager** beavers work very hard and try to please. What kind of work are you **eager** to do?

fuel (**fyoo**-uhl)

noun

Fuel is anything burned to make heat or power. Some kinds of fuel are coal, wood, oil, and natural gas.

Whose turn is it to gather more fuel for the fire?

WordWork

SAY: Food and water are the **fuel** our bodies need.

WRITE: Trucks burn more **fuel** than most cars.

DO: What kind of **fuel** heats your home? Your school? What **fuel** makes an airplane fly? What **fuel** makes a train run? Find out. Make a chart to show what you learn.

---

avoid (uh-**void**)

verb

Avoid means to keep away from something or someone. People often avoid things they don't like.

It's smart to avoid things that may hurt you.

WordWork

SAY: Another word for **avoid** is *dodge*.

WRITE: We can **avoid** the crowds if we leave early.

DO: You might be able to **avoid** a problem if you take special care. How can you **avoid** getting sunburn? What are some dangers you can **avoid**? How can you **avoid** them? Share your ideas with a few classmates.

giddy (gid-ē)
adjective

Giddy means dizzy or lightheaded. If you are giddy, you might feel like you are whirling or are about to faint.

When the nurse showed me the needle, I began to feel giddy.

WordWork

SAY: Another word for **giddy** is *unsteady*.

WRITE: I felt a bit **giddy** after the bouncy boat ride.

DO: Some people feel **giddy** when they swing too high on a swing. Others feel **giddy** when they climb a ladder. Have you ever felt **giddy**? What made you feel this way? Talk about it with a partner.

escape (i-skāp)
noun

An escape is a breakaway or getaway—it is a fast or sly way to become free of or avoid something unpleasant.

As soon as the bell rang, we made our escape from school.

WordWork

SAY: The guards learned that the prisoners had planned an **escape**.

WRITE: Reading is my favorite **escape** from doing chores.

DO: Have you ever made an **escape** from something or someone? What were you trying to break away from? Where did you go or what did you do to make your **escape**? Tell a classmate about your **escape**.

gape (gāp)

verb

Gape means to stare at something with your mouth wide open. It also means to be wide open.

The children gape at the large dinosaurs in the museum.

WordWork

SAY: We all **gaped** at the juggler's great skill.

WRITE: The birthday boy **gaped** at all of his gifts.

DO: **Gape** into a mirror. Then draw a picture of yourself **gaping**. Write about something that makes you **gape**.

---

perky (pur-kē)

adjective

Perky means cheerful and lively.

Perky people are often playful and fun-loving.

WordWork

SAY: Other words for **perky** are *merry* and *jolly*.

WRITE: We enjoyed watching the **perky** child sing a solo.

DO: Act out being **perky**. What can you do to show that you are feeling **perky**? What things can you say to make you sound **perky**?

Daily Vocabulary Boosters © 2011 by Marcia Miller & Martin Lee, Scholastic Teaching Resources

knack (nak)

noun

A knack is a special skill or talent. If you have a knack for something, you can do it easily although others might find it hard.

Mr. Jones has a knack for painting wild animals.

WordWork

SAY: Another word for **knack** is *talent*.

WRITE: She really has a **knack** for spelling.

DO: Some people have a **knack** for knowing just what to say. Others have a **knack** for doing math. Do you have a **knack** for doing something special? Explain.

---

recall (ri-kawl)

verb

To recall means to bring back into your mind. It also means to remember.

I recall the first time I met my best friend.

WordWork

SAY: Do you **recall** our trip to the pumpkin farm?

WRITE: I can't **recall** his phone number.

DO: How far back in time can you **recall** things in your life? Do you **recall** learning how to write your name? Riding a bike for the first time? Your first day of school? Draw three things that you **recall** from your younger days.

sturdy (stur-dē)

adjective

Sturdy means strong, solid, and firm. Sturdy things often hold up well, even when treated roughly.

Please sit in the sturdy chair.

WordWork

SAY: Other words for **sturdy** are *tough* and *well-made*.

WRITE: The painter uses a **sturdy** ladder.

DO: Why is it best to use a table with **sturdy** legs? What might happen if you try to eat a meal at a table that is not **sturdy**? Design a table on paper. Describe how you will make sure your table is **sturdy**.

---

effort (ef-ert)

noun

Effort means a strong try, or an attempt to do something. When you make an effort, you do your best.

It took great effort to climb to the top of the hill.

WordWork

SAY: Sometimes it takes a lot of energy to make an **effort**.

WRITE: Let's make an **effort** to be friendly.

DO: Think of things you tried to do today. Which things took great **effort**? Which ones took less **effort**? Which took almost no **effort**? Make a chart to compare the amount of **effort** it takes to do different things.

Daily Vocabulary Boosters © 2011 by Marcia Miller & Martin Lee, Scholastic Teaching Resources

discard (di-**skard**)
verb

Discard means to throw away or get rid of.

We discard things we don't want or need any more.

WordWork

SAY: Another word for **discard** is *scrap*.

WRITE: We **discard** empty bottles and cans in a recycle bin.

DO: Clean out your desk, locker, backpack, or cubby.
Make a pile of things you want to **discard**.
Why will you **discard** these things?
Explain your reasons.

risky (**ris**-kē)
adjective

Risky means full of danger. It can also
mean the possibility of failing at something.
Some risky things are unsafe.

High-speed racing is a risky sport.

WordWork

SAY: Think hard before making any **risky** moves on a skateboard.

WRITE: It is **risky** to be outside in a lightning storm.

DO: Some people use the saying "It's **risky** to put all your eggs
in one basket." Imagine carrying a heavy basket of eggs.
Why do you think this is **risky**? What do you think the saying
means? Share your ideas with classmates.

mound (mound)
noun

A <u>mound</u> is a small hill made of soil or rocks. It can also be a pile of things like money, paper, shoes, or trash.

In baseball, the pitcher throws the ball from a <u>mound</u>.

WordWork

SAY: Another word for **mound** is *heap*.

WRITE: We raked leaves into a big **mound**.

DO: Have you ever seen a **mound** of clothes or paper?
Have you ever made a **mound** of something?
Write about what you would do with a **mound** of money.

---

quench (kwench)
verb

<u>Quench</u> means to put an end to a thirsty feeling. It also means to stop, or put out. Firefighters <u>quench</u> flames with their water hoses.

Would you like some water to <u>quench</u> your dry mouth?

WordWork

SAY: Another word for **quench** is *douse*.

WRITE: We use lots of water to **quench** our campfires.

DO: What do you like to drink to **quench** your thirst?
Poll classmates to find out what thirst-**quencher** is the class favorite. Display the results in a graph or table.

Daily Vocabulary Boosters © 2011 by Marcia Miller & Martin Lee, Scholastic Teaching Resources

false (fawls)
adjective

False means wrong or not correct, like a false answer. It also means not real, like false teeth.

One of the model's false eyelashes fell off her eyelid.

WordWork

SAY: Other words for **false** are *fake* and *untrue*.

WRITE: If you make a **false** move, you may lose the game.

DO: Gather some friends to make two teams. Pick a topic, like math or spelling. Then play "True or **False**." The teams take turns making a statement about the topic. The other team must decide if it is true or **false**. If the team's guess is right, it gets one point. Have fun!

kennel (ken-l)
noun

A kennel is a place for raising and training dogs.

Jack puts his dogs in a kennel when he goes on vacation.

WordWork

SAY: Marcy calls her **kennel** "Doggie Camp."

WRITE: We picked up our new puppy from the **kennel**.

DO: Invite a **kennel** worker to your class. Or take a trip to a **kennel**. Plan questions you can ask, such as: "What jobs do people do at the **kennel**?"

confess (kuhn-**fes**)
verb

Confess means to admit that you did something bad or wrong. It means to tell the truth when questioned.

My brother had to confess that he broke the lamp.

WordWork

SAY: A person might **confess** to something by saying he or she "owns up" to it.

WRITE: I was afraid to **confess** that I had not read the book.

DO: An old story tells about young George Washington. He chopped down a cherry tree. It was hard for George to **confess** to his angry father. But he did. He said, "Father, I cannot tell a lie. I cut the tree." Act out this story.

---

greedy (**grē**-dē)
adjective

Greedy means eager for more and more money, power, or things. Often, greedy people want more than they need.

The big, greedy cat chased the kittens away from the feeding dish.

WordWork

SAY: Please try not to be **greedy**. Just take what you need.

WRITE: The **greedy** boy grabbed the biggest piece of pie.

DO: Make a list of **greedy** characters that you've learned about from books, movies, or TV. Why was each character **greedy**? Did the character's **greedy** ways help or hurt him or her? Share your thoughts with a friend.

Daily Vocabulary Boosters © 2011 by Marcia Miller & Martin Lee, Scholastic Teaching Resources

clutter (kluht-er)

noun

Clutter means messy or untidy. Where there is clutter, stuff is all over the place—things are not put away.

I can't find my homework in all this clutter.

WordWork

SAY: Another word for **clutter** is *disorder*.

WRITE: Please clear the **clutter** off the table so we can eat.

DO: Is your desk full of **clutter**? Is there **clutter** in your cubby or locker? Be a **clutter**-buster! Make the mess go away.

admit (ad-mit)

verb

Admit means to tell the truth after trying to keep it from someone. It can be hard to admit something.

When I admit I made a mistake, I always feel better.

WordWork

SAY: Another word for **admit** is *confess*.

WRITE: I **admit** that I did feel scared.

DO: You may wait a long time before you **admit** to something. Here's an example: "I must **admit** that broccoli really tastes okay." Come up with three different endings to this sentence: "I must **admit** that . . . ." Write your sentences and share them with a friend.

handsome (han-suhm)

adjective

Handsome means good-looking. Handsome is usually used to describe a boy or a man.

My dad is the most handsome man in the world!

WordWork

SAY: Another word for **handsome** is *attractive*.

WRITE: The frog turned into a **handsome** prince.

DO: Make a collage of **handsome** people, **handsome** buildings, or **handsome** animals. Cut pictures from catalogs and magazines.

---

concert (kon-surt)

noun

A concert is a musical performance. At a concert, people sing or play music.

The band held a concert to collect donations for the food bank.

WordWork

SAY: People who go to hear a **concert** are called the audience.

WRITE: We went to an outdoor **concert** at the park.

DO: Work together in small groups to practice for a class **concert**. Different classmates can sing, rap, or play instruments. When the groups are ready to perform, invite guests to the **concert**.

Daily Vocabulary Boosters © 2011 by Marcia Miller & Martin Lee, Scholastic Teaching Resources

bellow (bel-ō)

verb

To <u>bellow</u> is to shout or roar. When you <u>bellow</u>, the sound you make comes from deep down near your belly.

Did your uncle <u>bellow</u> with pain when he hurt his finger?

WordWork

SAY: The captain **bellows** orders to the firefighters so they can hear him.

WRITE: You might **bellow** if you get angry or hurt.

DO: What kinds of animals **bellow**? What kinds of animals cannot **bellow**? Make a chart. List examples of each kind of animal.

---

sketchy (skech-ē)

adjective

<u>Sketchy</u> means not complete or without many details. A <u>sketchy</u> idea is not clear. It isn't complete.

For now, I only have a <u>sketchy</u> plan for building a treehouse.

WordWork

SAY: Another word for **sketchy** is *fuzzy*.

WRITE: I have a **sketchy** memory of the book's plot.

DO: A *sketch* is a picture with few details. The word **sketchy** comes from *sketch*. Look at some sketches. What makes them **sketchy**? Describe details you would add to make the picture more complete. Then make a **sketchy** drawing of your classroom.

future (**fyoo**-cher)

noun

> Future means a time that is to come. It is time that lies ahead.

A woman tried to predict my future by looking at my palm.

WordWork

SAY: Something that has already happened is the past; something that hasn't happened yet is the **future**.

WRITE: In the **future**, you might be able to visit Mars.

DO: People often wish they could see the **future**. If you could see your **future**, how might it look? Draw a picture of something that might be in your **future**.

---

glance (glans)

verb

> Glance means to take a quick look. It doesn't take long to glance at someone or something.

I glance out the window every few minutes to see if my ride has arrived.

WordWork

SAY: Another word for **glance** is *peek*.

WRITE: I **glance** at my watch to check the time.

DO: Put five objects on a table. Cover them with a cloth. Take off the cloth for a few seconds so a friend can **glance** at the objects. Then cover them again. What does your friend remember from that **glance**?

nosy (no-zē)

adjective

Nosy means too curious about other people's business. This word comes from the way many animals poke their noses into things to explore or be curious.

The nosy dog was surprised to find out what was in the hole.

WordWork

SAY: It's good to be curious, but not to be **nosy**.

WRITE: My **nosy** brother read my story without asking.

DO: It's usually not polite to be **nosy**. Are you ever **nosy** about others? How do you feel when someone is **nosy** about you? Are there ever any good reasons to be **nosy**? Share your ideas with classmates.

uproar (up-rohr)

noun

Uproar means a big fuss with loud noise and confusion. Sometimes an angry crowd might cause an uproar.

Everyone was in an uproar over the decision to close the city park.

WordWork

SAY: A fun word for **uproar** is *hubbub*.

WRITE: The surprise guest sent our class into an **uproar**.

DO: Have you ever seen or read about an **uproar**? Describe the **uproar**. What caused it? How did people act? How did the **uproar** end? Share the details with a small group or the class.

swerve (swurv)

verb

Swerve means to change direction all of a sudden. When you swerve, you quickly turn left or right.

Dad had to swerve around the tree limb.

WordWork

SAY: Drivers might **swerve** to avoid hitting something in the road.

WRITE: We had to **swerve** through the crowds to get to the movie in time.

DO: You can **swerve** when you ride a bike. Skaters can **swerve**, too. Act out what it is like to **swerve**. Then talk about reasons why people **swerve**.

vacant (vā-kuhnt)

adjective

Vacant means empty or not filled.

I think that old, vacant house looks spooky.

WordWork

SAY: A phrase that means **vacant** is "not in use."

WRITE: The diner has only one **vacant** booth.

DO: When you get on a bus, which seats do you hope to find **vacant**? Why? What does it mean if there are no **vacant** seats on the bus? What will you do if you can't find a **vacant** seat?

Daily Vocabulary Boosters © 2011 by Marcia Miller & Martin Lee, Scholastic Teaching Resources

sunrise (sun-rīz)

noun

Sunrise is the start of a new day. At sunrise, the sun comes into view for the first time that day.

We got up early to look for deer at sunrise.

WordWork

SAY: Other words for **sunrise** are *daybreak* and *dawn*.

WRITE: The opposite of **sunrise** is *sunset*.

DO: What time is **sunrise** tomorrow where you live? Check a newspaper or the Internet to find out. Chart the time for **sunrise** for each day in the next full week. Write about what you notice.

tremble (trem-buhl)

verb

Tremble means to shake in quick motions. You might tremble if you are cold, afraid, weak, or nervous.

My knees tremble when I have to make a speech.

WordWork

SAY: An earthquake can cause the earth to **tremble**.

WRITE: The tiny lambs **tremble** in the snow.

DO: In *The Wizard of Oz*, the Cowardly Lion and the Tin Man **tremble**. Think of other stories in which one or more characters **tremble**. What makes the character **tremble**? Act out scenes from the story. Don't forget to **tremble**!

wilted (wil-tid)

adjective

Wilted means droopy or limp and bent over.

This wilted plant needs to be watered.

WordWork

SAY: Water the roses so they won't get **wilted**.

WRITE: **Wilted** lettuce is limp and has no crunch.

DO: Get two live flowers. Put one in a glass of water. Put the other in an empty glass. Which one do you think will get **wilted** first? Why? See if you are right.

victory (vik-tuh-rē)

noun

A victory is a win in a contest, game, or battle.

The baseball players celebrated their victory with a huge party.

WordWork

SAY: The opposite of **victory** is *defeat*.

WRITE: We were so proud of our **victory** in the spelling bee.

DO: People like to honor a **victory**. One way to do this is to have a parade. Draw a picture of a parade that celebrates a **victory**. Add lots of details.

Daily Vocabulary Boosters © 2011 by Marcia Miller & Martin Lee, Scholastic Teaching Resources

arrive (uh-rīv)

verb

Arrive means to reach a place at the end of or during a trip.

Our teachers always meet us when we arrive at school.

WordWork

SAY: The opposite of **arrive** is *depart*.

WRITE: The taxi will **arrive** at noon.

DO: Write a poem about how it feels to **arrive** home after you have been away for a long time. Use your imagination. Read your poem aloud to a small group or the whole class.

charming (charh-ming)

adjective

Charming means delightful or pleasing. A charming person is enjoyable to be around.

We stayed in a charming little cottage by the lake.

WordWork

SAY: Another word for **charming** is *appealing*.

WRITE: What a **charming** neighbor you are!

DO: How do you think Prince **Charming** got his name? Work with a small group to make up a skit about a king's very **charming** son. Then act it out for the class.

hinge (hinj)

noun

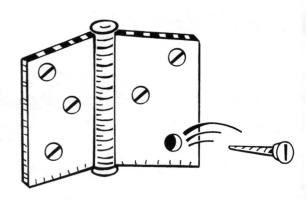

A <u>hinge</u> is a joint that holds two things together. The <u>hinge</u> allows one part to swing or to open and close. Most doors and gates have <u>hinges</u>.

We need to put one more screw into the <u>hinge</u>.

WordWork

SAY: A long time ago, people made **hinges** out of leather.

WRITE: Use oil to loosen that rusty **hinge**.

DO: Your body has **hinges** that are made of bone. Special tissues and muscles help them move. Your jaw is a **hinge**. Find your jaw **hinges** near the bottom of your ears. Feel them move as you open and close your mouth. Where are other **hinges** on your body?

ignore (ig-**nohr**)

verb

<u>Ignore</u> means to pay no attention to something.

The teacher tries to <u>ignore</u> me when I act silly.

WordWork

SAY: A phrase that means **ignore** is "tune out."

WRITE: Just **ignore** people who make rude comments.

DO: Never **ignore** a fire drill. It's important to know what to do in case of fire. Make a list of safety rules that you should never **ignore**. Share your list with the class.

scenic (sē-nik)

adjective

Scenic describes a view of a beautiful area of nature. A scenic place has a lovely setting.

On our boat tour, we enjoyed some scenic views of the mountains.

WordWork

SAY: They took a **scenic** drive along the coast.

WRITE: We took long, **scenic** walks around the lake.

DO: What kinds of **scenic** views do you like? Bring in photos or draw pictures of **scenic** places that you have visited or would like to visit. Describe your pictures to classmates.

---

ailment (āl-muhnt)

noun

An ailment is a sickness or illness. An ailment is not a serious problem, but it can bother you.

Lucy is very healthy, but she gets a minor ailment now and then.

WordWork

SAY: Dad wears a special brace for his back **ailment**.

WRITE: Mom gave me some medicine for my stomach **ailment**.

DO: Have your ever gone to the school nurse for an **ailment**? What sorts of **ailments** do school nurses treat? Invite a nurse to your class. Ask the nurse to tell which **ailment** is most common among school children. Ask any questions you might have about minor **ailments**.

nibble (**nib**-buhl)
verb

Nibble means to take little bites. When you nibble, you bite quickly and gently.

I watched the fish nibble at the bait on the hook.

WordWork

SAY: I like to **nibble** on carrot sticks.

WRITE: The mice **nibble** at the cheese.

DO: Rodents are known to **nibble**. Use books or the Internet to learn about rodents. Name some animals that are rodents. Find out what is special about their teeth and why they **nibble**. Share what you learn with a friend.

---

flimsy (**flim**-zē)
adjective

Flimsy means weak or thin. Some flimsy things are poorly built and may break easily.

It only took one puff of wind to blow down the flimsy straw house.

WordWork

SAY: Another word for **flimsy** is *fragile*.

WRITE: That bag is too **flimsy** to hold books.

DO: Look around the room for items that are **flimsy**, like tissue paper, thin fabric, and string or yarn. Notice how the items look and feel. How are some of these **flimsy** items used? Make a list.

Daily Vocabulary Boosters © 2011 by Marcia Miller & Martin Lee, Scholastic Teaching Resources

delay (di-lā)
noun

A <u>delay</u> is the period of time when something is late or is unable to happen. A <u>delay</u> can be caused by many things like weather, traffic, or illness.

The accident caused a long <u>delay</u> in our travel plans.

WordWork

SAY: Sometimes baseball games are stopped for a rain **delay**.

WRITE: We finally had our party after a weeklong **delay**.

DO: It's hard to know when you may have a **delay**. Pretend you are late for a party. List some possible reasons for your **delay**. Use your imagination!

---

invert (in-**vurt**)
verb

<u>Invert</u> means to turn upside down or flip over.

When you <u>invert</u> the letter H, it still looks the same.

WordWork

SAY: **Invert** the bottle to make the ketchup come out.

WRITE: If you **invert** the glass, it will dry faster.

DO: What happens if you **invert** letters and numbers? Make a two-column chart. On one side, list letters and numbers that look the same when you write them upright or **invert** them. On the other side, list those that look a different when you **invert** them.

rapid (rap-id)

adjective

Rapid means happening in a short time or very quickly.

The rapid rise in temperature melted most of the snow by noon.

WordWork

SAY: Other words for **rapid** are *fast* and *speedy*.

WRITE: Bamboo trees are famous for their **rapid** growth.

DO: When is your heartbeat more **rapid**: at rest or when you exercise? To find out, learn how to take your pulse. Take it when you are resting. Then run or jump for one minute and take your pulse again. Which of your pulse readings shows a more **rapid** heartbeat?

---

onset (awn-set)

noun

Onset means the beginning or starting point.

We want to get our flu shots before the onset of flu season.

WordWork

SAY: Another word for **onset** is *start*.

WRITE: The Pilgrims knew from the **onset** that their trip would be hard.

DO: What clues signal the **onset** of each season? Share your thoughts with a friend. Then draw a picture of things that signal the **onset** of your favorite season.

Daily Vocabulary Boosters © 2011 by Marcia Miller & Martin Lee, Scholastic Teaching Resources

expand (ik-**spand**)
verb

Expand means to spread out or become bigger. When some things expand, they swell in size.

Birds expand their wings to fly.

WordWork

SAY: Another word for **expand** is *enlarge*.

WRITE: Take a deep breath to **expand** your lungs.

DO: Some sofas can **expand** into beds. Think of things that can **expand** to do or be something else. Bring in examples or pictures. Show or tell how to make them **expand**.

knotty (not-ē)
adjective

Knotty means tricky or difficult, like trying to undo a lot of knots. A knotty problem can be complicated and hard to understand.

We drove through some knotty traffic to get around the closed road.

WordWork

SAY: Another word for **knotty** is *puzzling*.

WRITE: Let's solve this **knotty** problem together.

DO: Have you ever had a *knot* in your shoelace? Was it hard to undo? Picture this to help you remember what **knotty** means. Now try to solve a **knotty** puzzle or math problem.

glimpse (glimps)

noun

A glimpse is a quick look.

Did you catch a glimpse of the rainbow?

WordWork

SAY: Another word for **glimpse** is *glance.*

WRITE: I got a **glimpse** of the deer's white tail.

DO: You might get a **glimpse** of things as you travel past them. Take a pencil and pad of paper along the next time you ride in a car, bus, or train. List interesting things you catch a **glimpse** of while looking out the window. Later, share about some of your most unexpected **glimpses** with the class.

---

request (ri-kwest)

verb

Request means to ask for something. A request is usually made in a polite way.

What did you request from the dessert tray?

WordWork

SAY: Often, the thirsty runners **request** large bottles of cold water.

WRITE: We always **request** that our guests take off their shoes.

DO: Imagine you could **request** five new things for your class. Make a wish list. What would you **request** and why?

Daily Vocabulary Boosters © 2011 by Marcia Miller & Martin Lee, Scholastic Teaching Resources

drowsy (drou-zē)

adjective

Drowsy means sleepy or tired. When you feel drowsy, your eyelids may droop.

The baby gets drowsy when we push him in the stroller.

WordWork

SAY: Some medicine can make you feel **drowsy**.

WRITE: I felt **drowsy** after eating that big meal.

DO: How do you act when you are **drowsy**? Show a friend. How can you tell when someone else is **drowsy**?

atlas (at-luhs)

noun

An atlas is a book of maps.

We checked an atlas to find the location of England.

WordWork

SAY: How many times does our state appear in the **atlas**?

WRITE: We keep a road **atlas** in the car so we don't get lost.

DO: **Atlas** was a giant in Greek myth. The gods got angry at **Atlas** and made him hold the earth on his shoulders. Over 400 years ago, a famous book of maps was printed with **Atlas** on the cover. Soon a book of maps came to be known as an **atlas**. Can you find several **atlases** to compare?

insist (in-**sist**)

verb

Insist means to demand. When you insist on something, you stick firmly to what you want.

I insist that you take the first piece of cake.

WordWork

SAY: To **insist** means that you won't take "No" for an answer.

WRITE: I **insist** that you wear a bicycle helmet.

DO: Many families have rules that they **insist** every member must follow. What rules do people in your family **insist** on? Talk about them with a classmate.

---

gloomy (**gloo**-mē)

adjective

Gloomy means dark, drab, or dull. It also means discouraging or sad.

Is there anything I can do to make your gloomy mood go away?

WordWork

SAY: Another word for **gloomy** is *dreary*.

WRITE: The bats rested deep inside a **gloomy** cave.

DO: How do you feel when you wake up to a **gloomy** day? Draw a picture of how you look when you feel **gloomy**. Think of a **gloomy** song as you draw. Or play some **gloomy** music.

Daily Vocabulary Boosters © 2011 by Marcia Miller & Martin Lee, Scholastic Teaching Resources

delight (di-līt)
noun

A <u>delight</u> is something that gives joy or happiness.

What a <u>delight</u> the kids had at the water park!

WordWork

SAY: Another word for **delight** is *pleasure*.

WRITE: The circus was a **delight** for the whole family.

DO: Fourth of July fireworks are a **delight** to most people. What makes them such a **delight**? Write a story about fireworks you have seen. Give lots of details.

---

express (ik-**spres**)
verb

<u>Express</u> means to put thoughts into words. It also means to show thoughts through actions, without using words. You can <u>express</u> ideas by speaking, writing, or doing.

Her tears <u>express</u> her sadness and pain.

WordWork

SAY: What do you **express** when you smile?

WRITE: I want to **express** my thanks for the gift.

DO: There are many ways to **express** friendship. Write a poem, draw a picture, or tell a story to **express** how you feel about a special friend. Then share your *expression* of friendship with that friend!

thrifty (thrif-tē)

adjective

Thrifty means careful about spending money. It also means not being wasteful.

My thrifty neighbor uses large plastic butter tubs as plant pots.

WordWork

SAY: Uncle Phil is teaching me to be a **thrifty** shopper.

WRITE: A **thrifty** cook knows how to stretch a meal.

DO: **Thrifty** people don't spend money foolishly. **Thrifty** people try not to waste food, supplies, or anything else. In what ways are you **thrifty**? In what ways could you be more **thrifty**? Share your ideas with classmates.

center (sen-ter)

noun

The center is the exact middle. The center can also mean the main part of something, like the center of town.

Put the flowers in the center of the table.

WordWork

SAY: Other words for **center** are *hub* and *core*.

WRITE: The park is in the **center** of our neighborhood.

DO: Who sits nearest to the **center** of your classroom? Where is the **center** of the playground or gym? Figure out where the **center** is in different places at school. Share ideas to add to a class chart.

Daily Vocabulary Boosters © 2011 by Marcia Miller & Martin Lee, Scholastic Teaching Resources

wander (won-der)
verb

Wander means to move from place to place without direction or a plan. It can also mean to get lost, or to stray away from a path, place, or others.

Large herds of bison used to <u>wander</u> over the Great Plains.

WordWork

SAY: We can **wander** in the park until dinnertime.

WRITE: Does your mind ever **wander** during class?

DO: It can be fun to **wander** around a new place. As you **wander**, you might notice and learn new things. Where would you like to **wander**? Who would you like to **wander** with? Draw a picture and write a caption for it.

parched (parhcht)
adjective

Parched means dried out or very thirsty. A parched plant may have had too much heat or too little water.

The <u>parched</u> rabbit could not find water in the desert.

WordWork

SAY: I'm so **parched** that I could drink a gallon of lemonade.

WRITE: The long, dry summer left us with a **parched** corn crop.

DO: Death Valley is a desert in California. Look at pictures of Death Valley. How can you tell that it's a **parched** environment?

quarrel (kwarw-uhl)

noun

A <u>quarrel</u> is an argument or disagreement.
When people have a <u>quarrel</u>, they are often angry.

Jack didn't speak to Jill for days after their <u>quarrel</u>.

WordWork

SAY: Another word for **quarrel** is *spat*.

WRITE: The brothers had a **quarrel** over who would wash the dishes.

DO: It can be easy to get into a **quarrel**. But it's harder to end a **quarrel**. Talk with a classmate about how a **quarrel** might start and end. Together, act out a way to stop a **quarrel** between two friends who have lost their tempers.

vanish (van-ish)

verb

<u>Vanish</u> means to disappear suddenly or become invisible. Things that <u>vanish</u> go out of sight, maybe forever!

Did the bird <u>vanish</u> when you waved your wand over its cage?

WordWork

SAY: I saw the full moon **vanish** into the clouds.

WRITE: What made the dinosaurs **vanish** from earth?

DO: When magicians make things **vanish**, it's really a trick. But how do they do it? Read about magic tricks. Learn to make something **vanish**.

Daily Vocabulary Boosters © 2011 by Marcia Miller & Martin Lee, Scholastic Teaching Resources

nervous (ner-vus)

adjective

Nervous means feeling tense, uneasy, or jumpy. Some people might feel so nervous that they begin to tremble.

Fire makes most animals very nervous.

WordWork

SAY: Another word for **nervous** is *edgy*.

WRITE: I feel **nervous** before going to the dentist.

DO: "**Nervous** Nellie" is a term that describes someone who is especially tense or jumpy. Nobody really knows how this term got its start. Make up a story about **Nervous** Nellie to tell how she got her nickname.

distance (dis-tuhns)

noun

Distance means the amount of space between two places or things.

What is the distance between the two tall fence posts?

WordWork

SAY: "Keep your **distance**" means to stay far away from something or someone.

WRITE: The **distance** from my home to school is six blocks.

DO: You can use a yardstick or measuring tape to measure **distance**. Use one of these tools to measure the **distance** between your classroom and other rooms in your school. Use the map scale to find the **distance** between two places on a map.

insert (in-**sert**)

verb

Insert means to put, place, or fit into.

Insert the key into the slot to wind up the toy car.

WordWork

SAY: We need to **insert** two batteries into the camera.

WRITE: **Insert** a coin into the slot to buy bubble gum.

DO: Do you know how to **insert** a DVD or videotape into a machine to play a movie? Brainstorm things that can be used when you **insert** something into them. Think about things you come across at school, home, stores, or out in your community.

loyal (**loi**-uhl)

adjective

Loyal means being true or faithful. You can be loyal to a person, duty, country, or idea.

My dad travels all over the world, but he is loyal to his own country.

WordWork

SAY: Another word for **loyal** is *devoted*.

WRITE: True friends are **loyal** to each other.

DO: Dogs can be **loyal** pets. Have you ever read a story or watched a movie about a **loyal** dog? Tell a small group about how the dog showed that it was **loyal**.

Daily Vocabulary Boosters © 2011 by Marcia Miller & Martin Lee, Scholastic Teaching Resources

dwelling (dwel-ling)
noun

A <u>dwelling</u> is a house, apartment, cottage, or any other place someone might live in.

The old man's <u>dwelling</u> was a simple adobe house.

WordWork

SAY: Another word for **dwelling** is *home.*

WRITE: That **dwelling** is big enough for only one person.

DO: **Dwellings** come in all shapes, sizes, and materials. Make a collage of different **dwellings** from around the world. Find pictures in magazines, catalogs, or travel books. Use photos or postcards. Which **dwelling** would you like to live in the most? Share your ideas.

---

require (ri-kwīr)
verb

<u>Require</u> means to be in need of something. A person might <u>require</u> medicine to get well. <u>Require</u> also means to order or demand.

What poster size does the contest <u>require</u>?

WordWork

SAY: Call 9-1-1 if you **require** emergency help.

WRITE: Plants **require** water and light to grow.

DO: State laws **require** all drivers to pass a written and driving test. Should there be a law to **require** kids to pass a test before riding a bike? Share your thoughts with classmates. Then talk about what the test might **require**.

hazy  (hā-zē)

adjective

Hazy means covered with haze. Something that is <u>hazy</u> might look misty, foggy, or blurred. <u>Hazy</u> also means not very clear.

On a <u>hazy</u> day, it's hard to see things that are far away.

WordWork

SAY: July 4th this year was a hot, **hazy** day.

WRITE: I have only a **hazy** memory of our first house.

DO: It isn't easy to see well on a **hazy** day. How do **hazy** days cause trouble for some people? Share your thoughts with a friend. Then draw a picture of someone outdoors on a **hazy** day.

envy (en-vē)

noun

<u>Envy</u> is a jealous feeling. You feel <u>envy</u> when you want something that others have and are upset about not having it.

Sam talked about his <u>envy</u> over Mia's new car.

WordWork

SAY: Some people who feel **envy** might also be *greedy*.

WRITE: I felt a bit of **envy** when she won the award.

DO: Tell a friend about a time you felt **envy**. What made you feel **envy**? How did you get over your **envy**? Do you think anyone has ever felt **envy** over something you had or could do?

Daily Vocabulary Boosters © 2011 by Marcia Miller & Martin Lee, Scholastic Teaching Resources

collide (kuh-**līd**)

verb

Collide means to hit or bump into something with force. When things collide, something may get broken.

Oh my! Did you see the skateboarders collide?

WordWork

SAY: Another word for **collide** is *crash*.

WRITE: Kids **collide** their bumper cars into each other for fun.

DO: Airbags protect people if a car **collides** with something. Find out how an airbag works. Share what you learn with a small group. Then brainstorm other ways to keep safe in a car.

silent (**sī**-luhnt)

adjective

Silent means quiet or without sound.

The class became silent when the principal entered the room.

WordWork

SAY: Other words for **silent** are *still* and *hushed*.

WRITE: She stayed **silent** through the whole movie.

DO: Long ago, movies did not have sound. These are called **silent** movies. Have you ever watched a **silent** movie? Try this: Watch a movie on TV, but turn the sound down so you can't hear it. When it's over, write a review about the **silent** movie.

journey (jurn-ē)
noun

A journey is a long trip from one place to another.

Joe's journey began with a cruise across the ocean.

WordWork

SAY: We took a month-long **journey** through Italy.

WRITE: I'd like to take a **journey** into the past.

DO: A **journey** can be an adventure! Have you ever gone on a **journey** that turned into an adventure? Tell a friend about it. Then write and draw about your **journey**. Use your imagination to make your **journey** more exciting.

kindle (kin-dl)
verb

Kindle means to light up or set on fire. Kindle also means to stir up or excite, like when you kindle your hopes to win a game.

The park ranger taught us how to kindle a campfire using small twigs.

WordWork

SAY: Another word for **kindle** is *inspire*.

WRITE: Being in the play helped **kindle** my interest in acting.

DO: What is your favorite activity to do when you're not in school? Playing a sport or a game? Reading books or watching movies? What **kindled** your interest in the activity? Tell a few classmates about your favorite activity. Do you think you might **kindle** someone else's interest in it?

 Daily Vocabulary Boosters © 2011 by Marcia Miller & Martin Lee, Scholastic Teaching Resources

edible (**ed**-uh-buhl)
adjective

Edible means safe or fit to be eaten.

Did you know that some insects are edible?

WordWork

SAY: Are these **edible** berries or poisonous ones?

WRITE: Pick only the **edible** mushrooms.

DO: Many foods are **edible** even though you may not like their taste. Some foods are **edible** only after you cook them. Things that are not **edible** can make you sick. Learn about **edible** foods that grow wild near your home or community.

trophy (**trō**-fē)
noun

A trophy is an award or prize given to the winner of a contest. Often, a trophy looks like a fancy cup or statue.

Every member of our team got a trophy.

WordWork

SAY: The name of every player was on the silver **trophy**.

WRITE: Uncle Eric won a fishing **trophy**.

DO: Design a **trophy** for an imaginary contest. Use clay or pipe cleaners to make a model **trophy**. Add a label that tells what the **trophy** is an award for. Display your **trophy** model for others to admire.

increase (in-**krēs**)

verb

Increase means to add to something. Increase also means to make bigger or to grow in number or size.

Mom wants to increase the size of her garden next year.

WordWork

SAY: We want to **increase** our club membership.

WRITE: Will you please **increase** my allowance?

DO: How much do you think your height will **increase** by the end of the school year? Measure your height now. Then make a guess. Measure again at the end of the year. How much did your height **increase**? Was your guess close?

---

certain (**sur**-tn)

adjective

Certain means sure or without doubt. When you are certain about something, you know you are right.

Pam was certain her brother said to meet him in front of the school.

WordWork

SAY: Another word for **certain** is *positive*.

WRITE: Are you **certain** that the shop is open today?

DO: Make a chart with two columns. In one column, list some things that are **certain** to happen tomorrow. List things that are **certain** not to happen tomorrow in the other column. Share your chart with a small group.

Daily Vocabulary Boosters © 2011 by Marcia Miller & Martin Lee, Scholastic Teaching Resources

result (ri-**zuhlt**)

noun

A result is the effect or consequence of something.
The result of heavy rains could be flooding.

The tasty meal was the result of hours of cooking.

WordWork

SAY: Another word for **result** is *outcome*.

WRITE: If you put water in the freezer, the **result** will be ice.

DO: Scientists do experiments to learn the **results**. What will be
the **result** if you put a hard-boiled egg in a jar of vinegar?
Write down your guess. Then try it! Write the **result**.

compete (kuhm-**pēt**)

verb

Compete means to take part in a contest.
When you compete, you hope to do better
than all others.

My brother and I compete to see who runs faster.

WordWork

SAY: When you **compete**, you try very hard to win.

WRITE: We will **compete** in the checkers contest.

DO: Some people **compete** to win a prize. Others **compete** just for the
fun of it. What kind of things do you and your friends **compete** for?
Hold a math or spelling *competition* with a friend.

fragile (**fraj**-uhl)

adjective

Fragile means easily broken. You must handle fragile things with care.

Grandma keeps her fragile glass animals on a high shelf.

WordWork

SAY: Another word for **fragile** is *delicate*.

WRITE: Butterfly wings are **fragile** but beautiful.

DO: Think about the kinds of containers that eggs, glass, or other **fragile** items come in. What are they made of? How do they keep the **fragile** items safe? Write an imaginary tale in which you protect a **fragile** thing to keep it from breaking.

example (ig-**zam**-puhl)

noun

An example is used to show or explain something. A knife is an example of a cutting tool. An example is also something that can be imitated.

This costume is a good example of how a Pilgrim boy dressed.

WordWork

SAY: Another word for **example** is *model*.

WRITE: New York is a good **example** of a big city.

DO: Write an **example** of each of the following:
• A pair of numbers that have a sum of 100.
• A compound word that names an insect.
• An animal that can swim and fly.

Daily Vocabulary Boosters © 2011 by Marcia Miller & Martin Lee, Scholastic Teaching Resources

obey (ō-bā)

verb

Obey means to follow a law, a rule, or a request.
When you obey, you do as you are told.

We always obey the rules at the pool.

WordWork

SAY: Dogs can learn to **obey** simple commands.

WRITE: Safe drivers **obey** the traffic laws.

DO: A good citizen **obeys** the rules. In what ways are you
a good citizen in your class? Your school? Your community?
What rules are hard for you to **obey**?

honest (on-ist)

adjective

Honest means truthful. Someone who is honest
can be trusted.

An honest person would not lie, steal, or cheat.

WordWork

SAY: Another word for **honest** is *trustworthy*.

WRITE: Please give an **honest** answer to my question.

DO: Abraham Lincoln had a famous nickname. He was known as
"**Honest** Abe" because he believed in telling the truth. Why is
it a good idea to be **honest**? What might happen if someone is
not **honest**? Share your ideas with a small group or the class.

Daily Vocabulary Boosters Word List

admit (*verb*), page 63
agree (*verb*), page 51
ailment (*noun*), page 73
ajar (*adjective*), page 7
annoy (*verb*), page 29
arch (*noun*), page 27
arrive (*verb*), page 71
atlas (*noun*), page 79
avoid (*verb*), page 54

badge (*noun*), page 40
balk (*verb*), page 14
basic (*adjective*), page 46
bellow (*verb*), page 65
blaze (*noun*), page 16
brief (*adjective*), page 43
bulge (*verb*), page 15
bulky (*adjective*), page 44
burst (*verb*), page 32

calm (*adjective*), page 22
cease (*verb*), page 41
center (*noun*), page 82
certain (*adjective*), page 92
char (*verb*), page 12
charming (*adjective*), page 71
clutter (*noun*), page 63
collide (*verb*), page 89
commence (*verb*), page 30
compete (*verb*), page 93
concert (*noun*), page 64
confess (*verb*), page 62
core (*noun*), page 45
cozy (*adjective*), page 50
crane (*verb*), page 23
cross (*adjective*), page 16
crush (*verb*), page 45
cuddle (*verb*), page 48

damp (*adjective*), page 35
dawn (*noun*), page 18
delay (*noun*), page 75
delight (*noun*), page 81
depart (*verb*), page 47
dew (*noun*), page 25
dim (*adjective*), page 8
discard (*verb*), page 59
distance (*noun*), page 85
drift (*verb*), page 38
drowsy (*adjective*), page 79
dusk (*noun*), page 22
dwelling (*noun*), page 87

eager (*adjective*), page 53
edible (*adjective*), page 91
effort (*noun*), page 58
envy (*noun*), page 88
errand (*noun*), page 37
escape (*noun*), page 55
example (*noun*), page 94
expand (*verb*), page 77
express (*verb*), page 81

faint (*adjective*), page 25
false (*adjective*), page 61
fang (*noun*), page 48
feast (*noun*), page 49
flat (*adjective*), page 11
flimsy (*adjective*), page 74
fling (*verb*), page 42
flit (*verb*), page 17
fragile (*adjective*), page 94
fret (*verb*), page 44
fuel (*noun*), page 54
future (*noun*), page 66

gape (*verb*), page 56
giddy (*adjective*), page 55
glance (*verb*), page 66
glide (*verb*), page 26
glimpse (*noun*), page 78
gloomy (*adjective*), page 80
greedy (*adjective*), page 62
gruff (*adjective*), page 29

habit (*noun*), page 51
handsome (*adjective*), page 64
hazy (*adjective*), page 88
heed (*verb*), page 18
herd (*noun*), page 24
hinge (*noun*), page 72
hollow (*adjective*), page 49
honest (*adjective*), page 95

ignore (*verb*), page 72
increase (*verb*), page 92
insert (*verb*), page 86
insist (*verb*), page 80
invert (*verb*), page 75

jab (*verb*), page 8
jagged (*adjective*), page 47
journey (*noun*), page 90

kennel (*noun*), page 61
kindle (*verb*), page 90
knack (*noun*), page 57
knotty (*adjective*), page 77

lesson (*noun*), page 10
limit (*noun*), page 12
lone (*adjective*), page 13
loyal (*adjective*), page 86

meek (*adjective*), page 23
mend (*verb*), page 36
moist (*adjective*), page 31
mound (*noun*), page 60
mumble (*verb*), page 50

nervous (*adjective*), page 85
nibble (*verb*), page 74
nook (*noun*), page 7
nosy (*adjective*), page 67
notch (*noun*), page 39

oath (*noun*), page 36
obey (*verb*), page 95
onset (*noun*), page 76
oral (*adjective*), page 37

pact (*noun*), page 13
pale (*adjective*), page 14
parched (*adjective*), page 83
pause (*verb*), page 6
perky (*adjective*), page 56
plead (*verb*), page 39
pleasure (*noun*), page 30
plump (*adjective*), page 41
prop (*noun*), page 34
pure (*adjective*), page 17
purchase (*noun*), page 43

quarrel (*noun*), page 84
quench (*verb*), page 60

ramp (*noun*), page 15
rapid (*adjective*), page 76
recall (*verb*), page 57
remove (*verb*), page 24
request (*verb*), page 78
require (*verb*), page 87
result (*noun*), page 93
reveal (*verb*), page 53
risky (*adjective*), page 59

scenic (*adjective*), page 73
scowl (*verb*), page 35
selection (*noun*), page 46
shoo (*verb*), page 9
shred (*verb*), page 21
silent (*adjective*), page 89
sketchy (*adjective*), page 65
skull (*noun*), page 21
slick (*adjective*), page 28
sluggish (*adjective*), page 52
sly (*adjective*), page 19
spine (*noun*), page 31
sturdy (*adjective*), page 58
sunrise (*noun*), page 69
swamp (*noun*), page 33
swerve (*verb*), page 68
swift (*adjective*), page 26

tame (*adjective*), page 20
thaw (*verb*), page 20
thorn (*noun*), page 28
thrifty (*adjective*), page 82
tidy (*adjective*), page 34
tremble (*verb*), page 69
trophy (*noun*), page 91
trudge (*verb*), page 33
tuft (*noun*), page 6

unique (*adjective*), page 40
uproar (*noun*), page 67

vacant (*adjective*), page 68
vanish (*verb*), page 84
vast (*adjective*), page 10
victory (*noun*), page 70
vivid (*adjective*), page 32
vow (*noun*), page 9

wade (*verb*), page 11
wander (*verb*), page 83
wedge (*noun*), page 19
whirl (*verb*), page 27
wilted (*adjective*), page 70

youth (*noun*), page 42

zesty (*adjective*), page 38
zilch (*noun*), page 52